Climatology

The New Religion

By

Edward J Hahnenberg, MA,MA, Ed. S.

I got into the issue of Climatology with the purchase last year of a 2015 Nissan Leaf, a true EV, or electric vehicle. The Leaf is an acronym for "Leading, Environmentally, Friendly Affordable, Family car". I had some experience with a six month ownership of a Chevrolet Volt, but, all my life I had been the driver of gas powered vehicles. I drove several thousands of miles in vehicles, mainly Hondas.

Most of my travels were education related. I traveled to over half the states in the US, pursuing post-secondary credits at eleven colleges and universities. In so doing, I was able to secure careers in primary and secondary education in Michigan.

I would like to clarify some terms before delving into the substance of this book.

First: **Climatology**. It is the scientific study of climate, scientifically defined as weather conditions averaged over a period of time.

Second: **Religion**: There are about10,000 distinct religions worldwide encompassing a wide variety of academic disciplines, including theology, comparative religions, and social scientific studies

 Third: **Climate change**. Climate change is a change in the statistical distribution of weather patterns when that change lasts for an extended period of time

Fourth: **Global Warming.** It is a gradual increase in the overall temperature of the earth's atmosphere generally attributed to the greenhouse effect caused by increased levels of carbon dioxide, chlorofluorocarbons, and other pollutants.

Those who espouse climate change accuse the industrial world of "polluting" the climate, and they demand reparation (redress) for developing countries, which accounts for the "justice" in their "Climate Justice." Slavery, and the systematic subjugation of African Americans that followed it officially until the day before yesterday, was evil. Its legacy is evil. Its surviving remnants are evil. It is not an evil that is unique in the world — savagery and horror being the natural state of *H. sap.* — but it is an evil that is unique in the context of the United States of America. Its consequences remain very much with us, as anyone with eyes to see can discern.

Reparations are the wrong way to mitigate that evil. One reason for that is that reparations proposals are not intended to mitigate that evil. They are intended to make Elizabeth Warren, "professor of color," president of the United States. And, if not Warren, then Senator Harris, Senator Kirsten Gillibrand In a twitter statement Alexandria Ocasio-Cortez suggested a few more ways to gain traction: - "Support a Federal Jobs Guarantee - Bailout Student Debt - Legalize Marijuana & Explore Reparations…"

Their gospel, roughly put, is that the earth is warming perilously due to human activity. We must, therefore, limit this deadly, global menace. Never mind that "human-caused global warming" is a hypothesis, not a fact, and a weak one at that, given the mind-boggling scope of the premise, and the astonishing complexity of the data involved in the verification/validation of this hypothesis. Their devil is Carbon dioxide (CO_2). But CO_2 is essential to life on earth, and, number

of eminent scientists, CO2 levels do not
present any danger to our existence.

Chapter One: The Horror

According to the Intergovernmental Panel on Climate Change (IPCC) has failed to properly educate global leaders and has significantly underestimated timetables, which in turn has dangerously diminished awareness of the emergency we are in. In spite of 30 years of warnings by credible scientists and the work of the environmental movement, plus a preponderance of collaborating scientific evidence, as well as numerous conferences (21 to date,) and previous treaties, the carbon dioxide and methane pollution of the atmosphere has not stopped, slowed, or even leveled off. On the contrary, it is getting worse *faster than ever before!*

When I taught Global issues in high school, one of the debates I encouraged was the validity of the Kyoto Protocol of 1997. Many have asked why the US has not ratified the Kyoto Protocol on the reduction of greenhouse gas emissions. And why does the US continue to oppose drawing up binding agreements to reduce emissions?

Researchers at the Centre for International Climate and Environmental Research – Oslo (CICERO) have studied how the Kyoto negotiations unfolded 13 years ago, viewed in the context of the US political system. According to the researchers, the key to understanding why the US puts up roadblocks to a climate agreement is the way the US Congress is organised and functions.

Under the Kyoto Protocol industrialised countries agreed to reduce their greenhouse gas emissions by an average of 5.2 per cent by 2012 based on 1990 levels. The agreement entered into force in 2005 after being ratified by 127 countries. The US has not ratified the agreement.

"Just a few months before the UN climate change conference in Kyoto, senators in the US Congress unanimously adopted a resolution stating that the US should not be a signatory to any agreement that would mandate new commitments to limit or reduce greenhouse gas emissions only in industrialised countries or that would result in serious harm to the US economy. In the Republican-controlled Senate at that time, the Kyoto Protocol did not conform to either of these requirements.

Leading climate scientists like James Hansen, who originally warned us about the global warming danger 30 years ago, say we would remain safe if carbon in the atmosphere did not go over 350 parts per million (ppm). As of October 2017, carbon was near 409 ppm _ and increasing at about 4 ppm per year in a near exponential progression.

When you combine the heating effect of carbon with the other greenhouse gases, it is called the CO2e ppm rating. CO2e, or carbon dioxide equivalent. CO2e is a standard unit for measuring all greenhouse gases in terms of the amount of warming they create compared to CO2.carbon footprints.

When you **include atmospheric methane** and the other greenhouse gas pollutants, our current adjusted CO2e rating has already risen to the shocking level of 430 ppmv of CO2e! Worse yet, we will be at carbon 450 ppm in 10 years or less when we include atmospheric methane in our calculations.

To put this in a time-lapse perspective, from 1850 to about 1950, the increase in carbon pollution was steady at about 1 ppm per year. From 1950 to 2000, the increase rose to 2 ppm per year, and now in its current exponential curve, it is at about 3 ppm per year and rising rapidly toward 3-4 ppm per year. If carbon continues to rise in this exponential, nonlinear way, virtually unchecked by our ineffective previous actions, the increase could easily reach a level of 4 plus ppm per year by 2025.

According to James Hansen, a carbon 450 ppm level would eventually correspond and develop into an average global temperature increase of 6° Celsius (10.8° Fahrenheit) in this century and the end of human civilization as we've come to know it. Based on carbon ppm levels already in the system and reaching the 450 mark, this also means at least another 2.7° Celsius (4.9° Fahrenheit) global temperature increase beyond where we are now is the eventual and inescapable future reality.

This 2.7° Celsius would also be the most realistic minimal temperature increase to project as part of any future planning over the next 10-30 years. Bear in mind that even this scenario applies only if everything goes perfectly and we cross no additional global warming tipping points.

Unfortunately, it is highly probable that because of our ongoing denial and delay in addressing escalating global warming, atmospheric carbon parts per million will most likely continue to rapidly rise beyond the carbon 450-550 ppm total, which translates to a 3° to 4° Celsius increase (5.4° to 7.2°+ Fahrenheit) up to as much as a 6° Celsius (10.8° Fahrenheit) increase in average global temperature. (A 4° Celsius increase [7.2° Fahrenheit] in average global temperature would become "Hell on earth" as Mark Lynas, author of Six Degrees: Our Future on a Hotter Planet, has stated.)

Hansen's projections for "ending human civilization as we know it" are not the same as mass human extinction as we approach the 5° or 6° Celsius (9° to 10.8° Fahrenheit) temperature levels. In Hansen's 6° Celsius rise coming from eventually crossing the carbon 450 ppm mark, what would be considered normal, comfortable, or predictable daily life in developed nations will be severely impaired. In undeveloped nations, there will be a level of chaos and breakdown that will rapidly render most of these nations politically and economically unsustainable. As it is already occurring, the chaos of existing less-developed nations destabilized by factors such as war and the global warming emergency will affect the more developed and stable nations far beyond just the current massive migrations of those escaping the suffering.

In spite of all the media PR, 21 UN / IPCC international climate conferences, endless warnings from credible scientists over the last 30 years, and national reduction pledges and treaties, things are worsening in a nearly exponential progression (2,4,8,16, etc.). There is no way to deny we are not only losing the escalating global warming battle, but losing it at a progressively faster rate so that now global warming is now irreversible. Instead of enacting the needed changes when they were far easier, more gradual, and far less costly, we must now take radical, painful, and costly tough medicine if we are going to save the future. The changes that would have been inconvenient 30 years ago will now become nearly unbearable.

Some of today's most disturbing global warming facts

1. We are not receiving adequate accurate facts about how bad **escalating global warming** is now, or how bad it will become. The heavily fossil fuel lobbied major media conglomerates politely decline to alarm us about the real dangers of irreversible global warming emergency in order to allow the fossil fuel industry to continue *business as usual.*
2. Current atmospheric fossil fuel burning-related carbon ppm values are now at 409. This is higher than at any other time in the last 1 million years (possibly higher than any time in the last 25 million years). This new carbon pollution record represents an increase of 85 carbon ppm in the 55 years since David Keeling began making his revolutionary atmospheric carbon pollution measurements at Mauna Loa. (See graphs in this document.)
3. Carbon pollution accumulating in the atmosphere has been increasing even faster over the last few decades. It is

now nearly certain that if we refuse to take immediate, effective measures to resolve global warming, future increases will happen at *even faster rates*.

4. Global average temperatures have the potential to rise *far faster* than what we normally experience. For example, about 9600 BC,global temperatures rose 7° C (12.6° F) in less than a decade, pushing the ice sheets into rapid collapse and sending sea levels soaring.

Our 30-year inability to control the global warming emergency is due in part to:

1. The lack of national and international verifiable and enforceable international laws that would make continued large-scale carbon and methane pollution of the atmosphere a strongly punished activity or crime.
2. The physical time lags in developing and deploying the infrastructure needed for the new green energy technologies.

As we are progressing now, it will
likely take another 30-50 years.

If everyone and every government
simultaneously agreed to scale up green
energy generation immediately and there were
no budgetary or resource restrictions in
completing this life-critical project, it would
still take 30-50 years to put that infrastructure
in place. If escalating global warming and its
consequent climate destabilization, proceed to
the levels currently being predicted, it will
eventually cost the global society hundreds of
trillions of dollars in disaster recovery, as well
as soaring insurance rates, massive real estate
losses and depreciation, and massive coastal
and other infrastructure losses, in addition to
the vast amount of human suffering and death.

Right now, most nations are struggling with
debt and their economies are in trouble with
anemic annual growth. How will many of
these nations, particularly the weakest ones,
remain politically or financially viable, stable,
or even continue to exist if another 5% or
more of their total GDP is drained off each
year into the continually escalating costs of
global warming-caused climate
destabilization? Current estimates project all

global warming consequences will cost 10 percent and maybe far more of the world's total GDP by 2100The global warming emergency is already here! Its super-storms, flooding, seasonal disruptions, wildfires, heat waves, migrating insect infestations, and droughts will continue increasing in magnitude, frequency scale. According to a recent analysis from scientists at the National Center for Atmospheric Research (NCAR), The worst case projections for global warming may be the most likely."

The next battle now lies in
keeping irreversible global warming from rising to an extinction-level event where human-caused carbon dioxide and methane levels in the atmosphere push the global temperature increases to 4°-6° Celsius (7.2°-10.8° Fahrenheit) above preindustrial levels and beyond.

An already "baked-in" future of higher temperatures no matter what we do

A 2° Celsius (3.6° Fahrenheit) increase in global average temperature by year 2100 has been the official estimate of the Intergovernmental Panel On Climate Change

(IPCC). But it is low and overly optimistic. This 2° Celsius IPCC estimate is based on the operating premise that everything happening in the very complex and highly interconnected climate system will always work perfectly as predicted, in our favor, and no more known or unknown climate tipping points will be crossed.

Planning for everything to go perfectly is the perfect plan for failure, and there's a dangerous global warming shocker hidden within these low temperature estimates. The first wave of escalating global warming superstorms or "millennial storms" (storm severity levels that have not been seen for thousands or tens of thousands of years) will be coming much sooner than we are planning for. When you include crossing more of the critical global warming tipping points and adjust projections in evaluating the current climate data, it suggests all types of extreme weather such as millennial superstorms, super droughts, super floods, and super wildfires could begin replacing our current waves of extreme weather in as little as 15 to 30 years.

- It is highly probable carbon parts per million (ppm) in the atmosphere will rise beyond the carbon 550 ppm total, which translates to a 3° to 4°+ Celsius increase (5.4° to 7.2°+ Fahrenheit) in average global temperature—Hell on Earth. A 6° Celsius (10.8° Fahrenheit) increase is also a realistic projection, and it could occur long before 2100.

- If we resolve global warming, we also create a green Third Industrial Revolution. This will directly and indirectly create millions of new green energy-related jobs worldwide to replace lost fossil fuel industry jobs.

Does this sound familiar? This is the heart of the Green Movement espoused by the liberal, progressive Democratic Left, led, of course, by the 29-year old Alexandria Ocasio-Cortez. Alexandria Ocasio-Cortez has declared herself "boss" of the "Green New Deal." Maybe she can explain where the money will come from to pay its $93 trillion cost. Because taxing the rich won't even scratch the surface.

At an event on in March 2019, Ocasio-Cortez complained about criticism of the Green New Deal — much of it coming from her own party — that it's a pipe dream. Former Virginia Gov. Terry McAuliffe, for example, said that "there are things that are great goals, but are unrealistic."

Ocasio-Cortez's response: "Some people are like, 'Oh, it's unrealistic, oh it's fake, oh it doesn't address this little minute thing. And I'm like, 'You try! You do it.' 'Cause you're not. 'Cause you're not. So, until you do it, I'm the boss. How 'bout that?"

Try to do what? Come up with an equally unrealistic plan that would bankrupt the nation? Because that's precisely what the Green New Deal would do.

Green New Deal's Gargantuan Price Tag

A new analysis from the **American Action Forum** finds that the Green New Deal, as laid out by New York Rep. Ocasio-Cortez and

Massachusetts Sen. Ed Markey, would cost up to *$93 trillion* in the first ten years.

Remember, the GND isn't just about converting the entire U.S. energy supply to renewable energy in a decade and establishing a "zero emissions transportation system."

The plan also includes things like "guaranteed" federal jobs, "universal health care," and "food security."

Beyond the bumper-sticker labels, the grandiose plan is vague on any of the details. Still, the AAF, which is headed up by former Congressional Budget Office Director Douglas Holtz-Eakin, was able to rough out the 10-year costs for each of the proposals.

A zero-carbon electricity grid would cost $5.4 trillion, the AAF calculates. A "zero-emissions transportation system," an additional $1.3-$2.7 trillion. "Guaranteed green housing" will cost anywhere from $1.6 trillion to $4.2 trillion.

Despite the GND's name, it's the proposals that have nothing to do with climate change that cost the most. The price tag for a federal guaranteed jobs program could run as much as $44.6 trillion over the next decade. The "universal health care" plan? $36 trillion.

Cost Will Likely Be Higher

If anything, these are lowball estimates.

To calculate the cost of converting to 100% renewable energy, for example, the authors simply assume that no new transmission lines would be needed, and that much of the renewable energy would come from nuclear power. Neither is realistic.

The price tag for a nationwide high-speed rail system that could replace airplanes doesn't factor in the massive cost overruns endemic to every other government infrastructure project — and which are wrecking California's attempt to build its own bullet train.

The $36 trillion cost for "universal health care" is in line with other estimates for "Medicare for all." All told, the cost of the "green" part of the Green New Deal would run from $8.3 trillion to $12.3 trillion over the next 10 years, according to the AAF report. The rest of it would cost an additional $42.8 trillion to $80.6 trillion.

Let's put this in perspective. At the low end, the GND would *more than double* the size of the federal government.

At the high end — roughly $9 trillion a year — even taking *every single penny* earned by tax filers with adjusted gross incomes over $50,000 would *not be enough money to pay the costs*.

Looked at another way, economists expect the entire U.S. gross domestic product over the next decade to total $266 trillion.

More Than A Third Of GDP

That means the Green New Deal would account for up to 35% of the nation's economy from 2020 to 2029. That's on top of existing federal government programs, which already consume more than 20% of GDP each year.

To call this "unrealistic" is the understatement of the year. It would be cataclysmic.

What's most shocking about the Green New Deal, however, isn't the unprecedented economic destruction it would cause. Nor is the fact that it will do nothing to prevent "climate change" from happening. Nor the fact that a 29-year-old socialist and her legions of followers think this would be neat.

What's most shocking about the Green New Deal is that so many leading Democrats, many of whom very much hope one day to be president, are blindly embracing it.

Chapter Two: Do We Need Worry?

Multiple studies published in peer-reviewed scientific journals[1] show that 97 percent or more of actively publishing climate scientists agree[*]: Climate-warming trends over the past century are extremely likely due to human activities. In addition, most of the leading scientific organizations worldwide have issued public statements endorsing this position.

According to Alex Epstein writing for Forbes Magazine Jan, 6, 2015:

"If you've ever expressed the least bit of skepticism about environmentalist calls for making the vast majority of fossil fuel use illegal, you've probably heard the smug response: "97% of climate scientists agree with climate change" — which always carries the implication: Who are you to challenge them?

"The answer is: you are a thinking, independent individual--and you don't go by polls, let alone second-hand accounts of polls; you go by facts, logic and explanation.

"Here are two questions to ask anyone who pulls the 97% trick.

1. What exactly do the climate scientists agree on?

Usually, the person will have a very vague answer like "climate change is real."

Which raises the question: What is that supposed to mean? That climate changes? That we have some impact? That we have a large impact? That we have a catastrophically large impact? That we have such a catastrophic impact that we shouldn't use fossil fuels?

What you'll find is that people don't want to define what 97% agree on--because there is nothing remotely in the literature saying 97% agree we should ban most fossil fuel use.

It's likely that 97% of people making the 97% claim have absolutely no idea where that number comes from.

If you look at the literature, the specific meaning of the 97% claim is: 97 percent of climate scientists agree that there is a global warming trend and that human beings are the main cause--that is, that we are over 50% responsible. The warming is a whopping 0.8 degrees over the past 150 years, a warming that has tapered off to essentially nothing in the last decade and a half."

Further, the astute George Will had this to say:

The initial target of Democratic "scientific" silencers is ExxonMobil, which they hope to demonstrate misled investors and the public about climate change. There is, however, no limiting principle to restrain unprincipled people from punishing research entities, advocacy groups and individuals.

But it is difficult to establish what constitutes culpable "misleading" about climate science, of which a 2001 National Academy of Sciences report says: "Because there is considerable uncertainty in current understanding of how the climate system varies naturally and reacts to emissions of greenhouse gases and aerosols, current estimates of the magnitude of future warming should be regarded as tentative and subject to future adjustments (either upward or downward)." Did Al Gore "mislead" when he said seven years ago that computer modeling projected the Arctic to be ice-free during the summer in as few as five years?

The attorney general of the Virgin Islands accuses ExxonMobil of criminal misrepresentation regarding climate change. This, even though before the U.S. government in 2009 first issued an endangerment finding, regarding greenhouse gases, ExxonMobil favored a carbon tax to mitigate climate consequences of those gases. This grandstanding attorney general's contribution to today's gangster government is the use of law enforcement tools to pursue political goals — wielding prosecutorial weapons to chill debate, including subpoenaing private donor information from the Competitive Enterprise Institute, a Washington think tank.

The party of science, busy protecting science from scrutiny, has forgotten Karl Popper (1902-1994), the philosopher whose "The Open Society and Its Enemies" warned against people incapable of distinguishing between certainty and certitude. In his essay "Science as Falsification," Popper explains why "the criterion of a scientific status of a theory is its falsifiability, or refutability, or testability." America's party of science seems eager to insulate its scientific theories from the possibility of refutation.

The leader of the attorneys general, New York's Eric Schneiderman, dismisses those

*who disagree with him as "morally vacant."
His moral content is apparent in his
campaign to ban fantasy sports
gambling because it competes with the
gambling (state lottery, casinos, off-track
betting) that enriches his government....*

*These garden-variety authoritarians are
eager to regulate us into conformity with the
"settled" consensus du jour, whatever it is.
But they are progressives, so it is for our own
good.*

Chapter Three: The Calm

I come from a family of farmers. My grandfather was a descendant from German immigrants who migrated to the United States. It was the year of 1877 on May 2 that Frank first saw the light of day from his parents' log cabin. He was the fourth child of a family of ten girls and three boys. The homestead was located in Bingham Township, Leelanau County, Michigan.

His parents were German. His father Joseph came from Germany and his mother, Mary Schaub's birthplace was on North Manitou Island, Michigan. His small log cabin was completely surrounded by forest. The nearest neighbor was a mile away. Drinking water had to be carried three quarters of a mile and the best way of accomplishing this was to wear a wooden yoke across your shoulders, from which were hung two wooden buckets. When it rained the family would catch the rain that fell from the roof of the cabin into a barrel, as water was scarce.

There was a huge birch tree that stood in the back of the cabin and in the spring it would be tapped for its liquid sap. Interestingly, the sap was used in place of water for washing hands and faces and for doing dishes.

At the age of six, his parents sent Frank to a log schoolhouse in the woods, which was a couple of miles from their cabin. At the age of seven he was sent to St. Mary's school in Provement (now Lake Leelanau). There he was taught by the Dominican nuns. The Dominican sisters were present until 1970 (in the H.S.). I became the first lay principal in that year.

At age thirteen, Frank was taken out of school to work herding cattle on a farm during the summer. Throughout the winters, he worked in the timber woods, cutting logs and cordwood. Later he worked for neighbors 10 hours a day, making $.75 a day. He had to walk two miles to work.

Frank's father came from Germany at the age of twenty, looking for a chance to explore the

New World, and so it was with great interest that Frank read the following headlines which appeared in the papers in the year 1896 such as "Gold for the taking in Alaska", "The land of the midnight sun", "Gold in the Klondike", "Gold in Dawson city and on Bonanza Creek and El Dorado Creek" , "Gold in the grassroots".

Frank said to himself that all that was needed was courage. He reasoned that he could make a fortune in a few weeks, that this venture was for him.

About that time, friends of his father in Cleveland Ohio sent him a book about all the gold fields in Alaska, and they really wrote it up big. Soon after, a letter arrived from these people, asking him to go with them to Alaska and stating that they would furnish all the money that he would need

In the fall of 1896, Frank left home alone to meet three people in Cleveland whom he had never met. There were three of them. Dr. Effie Obermiller, her secretary, Elma Berg, and a 22-year-old architect from Gibbonsberg, Ohio. He was 20 years old and had never been further away from home than Traverse City, Michigan, which was 20 miles. Frank and his father's friends bought four tickets at $400 each from a German company in Chicago. These tickets were to take them to Dawson city. Joseph Buchman from Gibbonsberg, was to be his partner.

Frank went to Seattle, Washington, where the other two members were to meet Frank and Joseph in February 1897, but upon arriving in Seattle, the two men found that they could not come until later. While waiting for them, Frank and his partner went to a mining school where they took a course in mining which taught them how to get gold out of frozen ground. Twice a week, Frank would play the violin at a dancing school. This helped to cover his living expenses while waiting for the rest of their party.

They found out that the company which had sold them the tickets for Alaska was a fake, so each of them lost $400. But, when Dr. Effie arrived, she informed Frank that she had plenty of money to stake all of them for the trip to Alaska.

It was in the early spring of 1897 that they purchased a complete outfit which consisted of 4000 pounds of food and 1000 pounds of equipment to use in mining. Everything they took in the line of food had to be frost-proof and put in waterproof bags. Most of the food was dried and dehydrated. Sugar, milk, and vinegar all came in small pills.

After outfitting themselves completely, they bought their tickets to Haines, Alaska on the steamer *Alice Blanchard* . Two days later the papers came out with the headlines: "Gold, Gold from the Klondike." The night before, the steamer *Excelsior* had arrived in San Francisco with $750,000 worth of gold dust from Scagway, Alaska and two days later the steamer *Portland* arrived in Seattle with over $90,000 worth of gold. Gold from the Klondike   that did it. That made the gold crowd crazy. Food prices went out of sight,

the fares went sky high. It was all
unbelievable.

Anyway, my father ,Fred, along with my
grandfather, Simon Hahnenberg, planted a
cherry orchard in the 1930's in a valley on an
80 acre plot of land Simon had purchased
prior to WWI. The land lies in the "little
finger" of the lower portion of Michigan, in
Leelanau County. The temperature was so
warm during the duration of the next 25 years
that the crops were abundant. Later on, in the
1990's, frost was always a concern in the
orchard I planted to replace the original one.
A frost in May could, and did, destroy an
entire crop because tart cherry blossoms can
only tolerate temperatures of 26 degrees for
an hour, before one can say good-by to that
year's crop.

In the "warm period" of the thirties, my dad
told me they planted oats in March!

Today, as I write this in March 2019, we have
three feet of snow in the same valley.

Also, the entire country has gone through one of the coldest winters in my memory .Polar Vortexes, with arctic storms, one after the other have put a strain on schools across the nation. In Michigan, some schools have cancelled classes up to thirty times, and we are still in the first week of March.

Another point: I am a fan of Tony Venture and his videos on his boats Venture I and Venture II.

According to Venture, who made his money by designing boats, he did some quite extensive cruising – mainly in Norway and other parts of Scandinavia - in an early Fleming 55 owned by the person who is now our agent in Australia. He had a GB42 in Singapore which he took to the Tioman Islands in the South China Sea off the east coast of Malaysia. That boat is under new ownership and now lives in Seattle.

As far as Flemings are concerned, he has owned two. Both have been 65's.

The reason I mentions the videos of Venture is because he did a lot of sailing in Alaska.

There are **616** officially named glaciers in Alaska (see USGS Geographic Names Information System online data base), and many more unnamed glaciers. The Alaska Almanac estimates that Alaska has **100,000 glaciers** -- that's a pretty good estimate.

In one of his adventures, Venture noted that a glacier discovered in the late seventeen hundreds has receded before any records of global warming were kept.

DAWES GLACIER

As we penetrated deeper up the 40-mile length of Endicott Arm, the sides of the fjord grew ever steeper until they became sheer rock walls bearing the scars of the glacier that had ground its way past them not so long ago. We encountered increasingly large quantities of ice calved from the Dawes Glacier. We kept going despite ominous thumps and bangs as the hull came into contact with the floes. Our perseverance was rewarded when the ice unexpectedly opened up and we reached open water.

Venture in the foreground with the falls running off of Ford's Terror behind her. The glacier face now appeared to be only a few hundred yards away but the radar showed it still to be 3 miles distant. Nothing remained in the way of our reaching the towering wall of ice, but discretion made us call a halt while we were still several hundred yards away. It was as well we did because large slabs of ice were calving from its blue, deeply fissured face.

Under improving weather we launched the tender, and my friend Louisa Chen and I climbed aboard, armed with cameras. Conklin ran Venture back and forth across the face of the glacier while I took photos and video. On one occasion, I heard a sharp boom coming from one end of the glacier and I held a video camera on that area. Increasingly, large chunks of ice started to break free followed by a large slab, which slid into the sea with a tremendous splash just as Venture entered the frame. Large swells resulted from this collapse but they were smooth and rounded and did not create a hazard.

It was hard to tear ourselves away from this amazing spectacle, but after an hour or so, we reluctantly turned our bows and threaded our way back out through the pack. We stopped to collect some crystal clear ice to cool our drinks.

Bald Eagle spotted near Juneau.
Our reluctance to leave the glacier had put us behind schedule and it was one hour past high water slack when we reached the entrance to Ford's Terror. The out-going tide was beginning to gather speed, but with the powerful engines we had at our disposal, we had no problem negotiating the narrow entrance. The guidebooks tend to dwell on the alarmist name and the perils of the entrance rather than what lies in store once past the

narrows, so the stunning beauty of the wonderland within came as a revelation. We had not appreciated, from reading the cruising guides, the outstanding nature of this magical place which was akin to cruising through Yosemite Valley.

To our surprise we found Penguin, a Nordhavn 46, whose crew we had met and come to know much earlier in the trip, already anchored at the head of the northern arm of the fjord together with their friend in a Nordic Tug. Care needs to be taken when anchoring here as depths drop off rapidly and you could find yourself aground at low tide if you have not watched the depth sounder and paid attention to the tide tables. The only sounds in this exquisitely beautiful spot were those of the nearby waterfall.

The following morning dawned absolutely calm with filaments of cloud lingering in the still air part way up the peaks. A flock of colorful Harlequin Ducks scavenged in the outfall from the waterfall. We launched the tender and explored the fjord. We passed through rapids guarding the eastern arm of Ford's Terror and then down to the main entrance to the fjord, which we sped through without any problem at low water slack. On the return journey, we poked our bows into a narrow cleft in the cliffs, through which cascading waterfalls tumbled over moss-clad rocks into water the color of jade. That evening we enjoyed a delightful evening aboard Penguin sharing drinks, conversation and tasty hors d'oeuvres.

In a boat the size of Venture, it is safer and more sensible to enter and leave Ford's Terror at high water slack, which occurs just twice in every 24 hours. This meant being underway at 5:30 the following morning. It was another opportunity too good to miss and I decided to go in the tender to take video and photos of Venture underway and passing through narrows.

The passing of time on display in the untouched rock faces of Ford's Terror.

I had a great run all the way down through the spectacular fjord and sped out through the narrows ahead of Venture, so that I could film her passing through. A beautiful chunk of floating ice added drama to the scene. Although the sky was overcast, there was no rain, which would have made photography very difficult. Just beyond the entrance, Venture resembled a toy against the background of a spectacular, multi-branched waterfall.

Penguin left at the same time and we both headed for Taku Harbor where there was a

*single sailboat tied up at the government dock
when we arrived just before noon. When we
left the following morning, a pair of
humpback whales were bubble-feeding just
outside the bay—rising up and bursting
through the surface of the sea with their huge
mouths agape. Unfortunately, they were too
far away for decent pictures, but it was a
memorable sight.*

*Just north of here we came across many sea
lions lounging on the rocks in Slocum Bay
before heading up Gastineau Channel leading
to Juneau. We arrived at the Intermediate
Dock at noon and tied up between two large
cruise ships. After several days of being
completely out of touch, it was a relief to be
able to connect to email and the Internet.
Communications all along this coast were
very sparse and unreliable.*

*Sawyer Glacier off Venture's bow. nearly
everywhere you look the eyes are met with
intense beauty.*

*Juneau is the capital of Alaska and, like
Ketchikan, the downtown area is dominated
by huge cruise ships, which come and go
every day. After a couple of nights moored
among the behemoths, we relocated to
cheaper Aurora Harbor further away from the
center of town and used the savings to rent a
car, which is strongly recommended if you
plan to spend any time in the capital of
Alaska. We took a ride up the Mount Roberts
aerial tramway but the low-clinging clouds
obscured the view. The last time we came
here in August of 2006, it rained every day for
three weeks. We were told at that time that we
needed to visit Juneau before July. This time
we are here in June and it is still raining!*

*We had a change of crew in Juneau. Christine
left us and we were joined by Australians
Peter and Bernie McMorrow, who had*

recently driven their Fleming 55 from Sydney to Perth—a journey of at least 6,000 miles across the top of Australia. Before departing Juneau we visited the Mendenhall Glacier, which, despite being a major tourist attraction, retained its grandeur and ability to impress. Arctic Terns, nesting in the area, flitted about our heads. These birds migrate every year from the Arctic to the Antarctic and back—a round trip of about 44,300 miles!

Here Venture is dwarfed by a massive cruise ship in Juneau.

From Juneau we continued on to Glacier Bay, for which you need a permit before entering the park. You cannot reserve your spot more than six weeks ahead of the intended date of your visit but, to ensure your preferred dates, it is best to make your reservation as soon as possible after that. En route we stopped at Gustavus from where we took a breathtaking charter flight over Glacier Bay before piloting Venture into its icy waters.

We spent three days cruising within the bay itself—reaching our maximum northing just shy of 60 degrees in the waters off Margerie Glacier. We were favored with wonderful weather. From here we turned our bows south and made our way back to Vancouver by way of Sitka and the "outside" Inside Passage. But that is another story!

Chapter Four: The Facts

I am an amateur astronomer and astrophotographer. I have photographed hundreds of nebulae and galaxies. Some samples: Below the Crescent nebula.

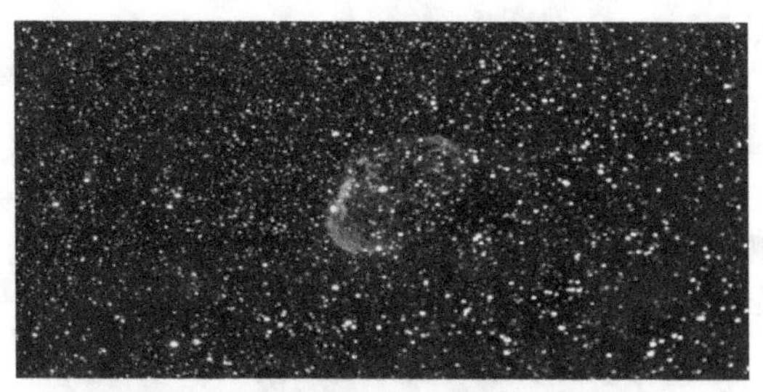

And the Horsehead nebula:

:

One of the things I have learned is that the earth's tilt relative to the sun is **23.5 degrees relative** to our orbital plane – the plane of Earth's orbit around the sun. The tilt in the axis of the Earth is called its obliquity by scientists.

I have also learned that because of this tilt, ice ages occur every 11,000 years or so. This has been going on for millennia. At
least **five** major ice ages have occurred

throughout Earth's history: the earliest was over 2 billion years ago, and the most recent one began approximately 3 million years ago and continues today (yes, we live in an ice age!). Currently, we are in a warm interglacial that began about 11,000 years ago.

There are several proofs of this:

Today the frozen Antarctic ice sheet borders the Southern Ocean. But tropical **palm trees** once flourished there. An intense warming phase occurred 52 million years ago, leading tropical vegetation, including palms and relatives of today's tropical **Baobab** trees, to grow on the continent's now frozen coasts.

Another is under glaciers in Alaska.

Ancient 1,000-Year-Old Forest Revealed Beneath Melting Alaskan Glacier

An ancient 1000-year-old forest has been uncovered beneath Alaska's 37 square mile **Mendenhall Glacier**. The forest has been poking through the receding ice near Juneau for nearly fifty years, but local scientists from the **University of Alaska Southeast** have observed an increasing number of visible stumps lately – including some trees that are still in an upright position.

There are many scientists who disagree with the conclusions drawn from VP candidate Al Gore's blockbuster book "An inconvenient Truth" It was made into a documentary in 2006. The premise is as follows:

Humanity is sitting on a time bomb. If the vast majority of the world's scientists are right, we have just ten years to avert a major catastrophe that could send our entire planet's climate system into a tail-spin of epic destruction involving extreme weather, floods, droughts, epidemics and killer heat waves beyond anything we have ever experienced- a catastrophe of our own making. If that sounds like a recipe for serious gloom and doom -- think again. From director Davis Guggenheim comes the Sundance Film Festival hit, "An Inconvenient Truth," which offers a passionate and inspirational look at one man's commitment to expose the myths and misconceptions that surround global warming and inspire actions to prevent it. That man is former Vice President Al Gore,

*who, in the wake of defeat in the 2000
election, re-set the course of his life to focus
on an all-out effort to help save the planet
from irrevocable change. In this eye-
opening and poignant portrait of Gore and
his 'traveling global warming show,' Gore
is funny, engaging, open and downright on
fire about getting the surprisingly stirring
truth about what he calls our 'planetary
emergency' out to ordinary citizens before
it's too late.*

Well, it has been ten years since Gore's dire
warning, and I don't see any major
catastrophe that is sending our planet into
epic destruction.

Chapter Five: The Deniers

The following information is largely drawn
from the Competitive Enterprise Institute:

*If we use the most accurate model, called
INM-CM4, and run it with a realistic
emissions scenario in which natural gas
continues to replace coal as an electricity*

fuel, the world warms about 1.5°C by 2100. In other words, humanity achieves the Paris climate treaty's maximum goal but without any additional climate policies. Climate change is not "worse than we thought," but better than they told us.

Because global temperatures are not spinning out of control, it is not surprising there have been no long-term trends in the frequency and severity of droughts and floods, in the frequency and strength of land-falling hurricanes, or in measures of total hurricane strength.

Despite relying on climate models that run too hot, the IPCC's Fifth Assessment Report tacitly rejects the catastrophe narrative popularized by Al Gore and other climate campaigners. Specifically, the IPCC concludes that in the 21st Century, Atlantic Ocean circulation collapse is "very unlikely," ice sheet crackup is "exceptionally unlikely," and catastrophic release of methane from melting permafrost is "very unlikely."

Social Benefits of Carbon

Besides, so-called carbon pollution has significant and well documented ecological and food security benefits. That's because rising CO_2 concentrations enable plants to grow faster and larger and use water more efficiently, and warming lengthens **agricultural growing seasons.**

In 2016, a team of 32 researchers from 24 institutions in eight countries used NASA satellite data to measure changes in "leaf area index, or amount of leaf cover, over the planet's vegetated regions" during 1982-2015. **They found** *an "increase in leaves on plants and trees equivalent in area to two times the continental United States." The CO2 fertilization effect accounts for* <u>70 percent</u> *of the greening trend, with nitrogen deposition (another fossil-fuel byproduct) and anthropogenic warming accounting for 17 percent. Has any climate policy done even a small fraction as much good for the planet?*

Climate researcher **Craig Idso**, *using a large database on carbon dioxide-enrichment experiments and Food and Agriculture Organization economic data, estimates that CO_2 emissions added \$3.2 trillion to the value of global agricultural output since 1961. Has* *any climate policy done even a small fraction as much good for people?*

Fossil Fuels Make Us Safer

Perhaps the most important reason trends in human well-being are improving despite climate change is that wealth creation and technological innovation make societies better able to manage climate-related risks. For example, since 1990, weather-related losses as a share of global GDP declined by about one-third. Since the 1920s, climate economist Indur Goklany reports, global deaths and death rates related to extreme weather decreased by 93 percent and 98 percent, respectively.

As fossil fuel consumption increased, the environment became more livable and human civilization more sustainable. That's not a coincidence. Energy scholar Alex Epstein explains: Human beings using fossil fuels did not take a safe climate and make it dangerous; they took a dangerous climate and made it safer.

For example, for millennia, drought was the most lethal form of extreme weather because it limits access to food and water. Since the 1920s, global deaths and death rates related to drought decreased by 99.8 percent and 99.9 percent, respectively.

That's largely the result of fossil fuel-supported technologies and capabilities: mechanized agriculture, synthetic fertilizers, refrigeration, plastic packaging, motorized transport, modern communications, and the economic surpluses that enable wealthier societies to aid poorer societies in times of distress.

Perils of Climate Policy

Climate campaigners hype the risks of global warming and belittle, ignore, or deny the benefits of fossil fuels. Would their so-called climate solutions—carbon taxes, cap-and-trade, renewable energy quota, fracking bans—make us safer or the reverse?

Pick almost any climate policy on the books, and you will find an abysmal benefit-cost ratio. For example, the Obama administration's Clean Power Plan would

*avert less than two-hundredths of a
degree Celsius of global warming by 2100.
That's according to the EPA's climate
simulator, a model aptly named MAGICC. Yet
achieving that miniscule result would
cost tens to hundreds of billions of dollars in
compliance burdens and economic fallout.*

*The stock rejoinder is that if the whole world
implements such policies, we can take big
bites out of global warming. Perhaps, but
then the problem is that any truly ambitious
global program of fossil-fuel suppression is
potentially a humanitarian disaster.*

*For example, according to the IPCC's
overheated climate models, the Paris
Agreement's central goal, which is to keep
global warming below 2°C, will require
reducing global carbon dioxide emissions 40-
70 percent below 2010 levels by 2050. There
is no known way to do that without
compelling developing countries to
make substantial reductions in
their current consumption of fossil fuels.*

*More than 1 billion people in developing
countries have no access to electricity and*

billions more have too little to sustain development.

Putting energy-starved peoples on an energy diet would trap millions in poverty and slow the march of progress to a cleaner, healthier, more peaceful world. It is a cure worse than the disease. Consequently, developing countries will not consent to implement it.

Unfortunately, vast resources may be diverted from far more beneficial investments before climate change loses its mystique as a pretext to expand government and empower progressive elites.

It is noteworthy, that 31,487 American scientists signed a petition,
including 9,029 with PhDs, which urged the US to reject the Kyoto Protocol in 1997, stating, in part, that "There is no convincing evidence that human release of carbon dioxide, methane, or other greenhouse gases will, in the foreseeable future cause catastrophic heating of the Earth's atmosphere and disruption of the Earth's climate."

The following is published by SAGE, The American Behavioral Scientist:

Climate Change Denial Books and Conservative Think Tanks

Exploring the Connection

Monitoring Editor: Riley E. Dunlap

Although just one of many forms of media employed by CTTs, books are especially important for reaching the conservative movement's core constituency, wider segments of the public, and critical sectors of society such as corporate, political, and media leaders. Books confer a sense of legitimacy on their authors and provide them an effective tool for combating the findings of climate scientists that are published primarily in scholarly, peer-reviewed journals—at least within the public and policy (as opposed to scientific) arenas. Authors of successful books critiquing climate science often come to be viewed as "climate experts," regardless of their academic backgrounds or scientific credentials, and despite the fact that their books are seldom peer reviewed. They are interviewed on TV and radio, quoted by newspaper columnists, and cited by sympathetic politicians and corporate figures. Their books are frequently carried by major bookstore chains, where they are seen (even if not purchased) by a wide segment of the public, many receive enormous publicity on CTT websites and from conservative and skeptical bloggers, and some are carried by the Conservative Book Club. In short, books are a potent means for diffusing skepticism concerning AGW and the need to reduce carbon emissions. Given the critical role of CTTs in challenging climate science and policy making, and their proclivity for using books to promote their causes, we expect to find a strong link between CTTs and books espousing climate change denial.

In part this expectation is based on prior experience. In an earlier study of environmental skepticism writ large (Jacques et al., 2008), we examined 141 books espousing skepticism toward the scientific evidence for environmental problems of all types (including global warming) published through 2005, looking for evidence of linkages to CTTs. We found that 130, or 92%, of the books were linked to a CTT, either via publication by a CTT press or a verifiable connection between the author or editor and a CTT, or both. These links to highly influential and generally well-heeled CTTs challenge a common theme of the books—namely, that the authors or editors are little Davids battling the Goliath of environmental science.

The present study extends our earlier work by examining books espousing climate change denial per se published through 2010, including some examined in the prior study since they represent examples of environmental skepticism. Besides focusing on book connections to CTTs, we also examine the educational credentials and national backgrounds of their authors or editors. Given that climate change denial has become widespread within the United States and to some degree internationally, we pay particular attention to the role of CTTs in diffusing a skeptical view of climate change and climate science to a wider audience both within the United States and internationally.

The Study

Our data set consists of the population of English-language books assigned an International Standard Book Number (ISBN) that espouse various forms of climate change denial. These books reject evidence that global warming is occurring, that human actions are the predominant cause of global warming, and/or that global warming will have negative impacts on human and natural systems. These arguments have been labeled trend, attribution, and impact denial (Rahmstorf, 2004). Books were included only if they take one or more of these positions challenging climate science, all of which are used to reject the necessity of carbon emission reductions. We located 108 books espousing one or more of these versions of climate change denial published through 2010, employing searches via online book stores, bibliographies in denial books, references in articles written by climate change skeptics, and several skeptic blogs that promote denial literature. Climate change denial books, especially those that were published by obscure presses or were self-published, can be difficult to locate, and we have possibly missed a few. However, we are confident that the 108 we analyze represent virtually all denial books in English, allowing us to generalize our findings with confidence.

We limit our analysis to first-edition books, ignoring the small number of second-edition volumes that came out in only slightly revised form.[2] The books are listed in the appendix (along with selected information we will shortly describe), grouped by their country of origin as determined via the lead author's or editor's apparent place of residence, and then arranged alphabetically by lead author or editor.

In addition to examining book links with CTTs—as done in our prior study—and location of lead author, we coded date of publication, the type of publisher employed, and information on the academic credentials (degrees and fields of study) of authors or editors. Our overall goal is to provide a good sense of the sources of these volumes—who is writing them and who is publishing them—paying special attention to the role of CTTs in the process. In the following sections we describe our coding decisions and thereby clarify information presented for each book in the appendix.

Results

We begin by charting the publication of these books over time, documenting the recent rapid increase in their numbers, and then highlight a significant new development—the growth of self-published books, often by laypersons denying AGW. We then examine the connections between CTTs and the books, noting how this connection differs for books issued by publishing houses and those that are self-published. We next examine the national origins of the books, showing how production of climate change denial volumes has spread from the United States to several other nations as denial has diffused internationally, noting the role of CTTs in this process. Then we turn to the academic and scientific credentials of the authors or editors of the books, highlighting trends over time and variation across nations. We end by commenting on how the publishing sources used by the denial authors enables most of them to avoid peer review.

Trends Over Time

The first denial volume, Sherwood Idso's *Carbon Dioxide: Friend or Foe*, appeared in 1982, well before AGW had achieved a prominent place on the nation's agenda. Highlighting the benefits of carbon dioxide, Idso took issue with early climate science that suggested increasing levels of carbon dioxide could produce deleterious effects. The remaining 107 books began appearing in 1989, the year after AGW became a highly visible issue in the United States and the IPCC was established, with 4 coming out that year. They were followed by 19 denial books published in the 1990s, 13 of them in the last half of that decade, reflecting a relatively slow but steady growth in their rate of publication. Another 15 appeared during the first half of the next decade, followed by a veritable explosion of 54 in the second half (especially 2007 to 2009), making a total of 69 from 2000 to 2009. Another 15 came out in 2010, yielding the total of 108 we are examining.

Conclusion

There is little evidence that global warming is having any serious effect on the Earth. Nobel prize winner Ivar **Giaever** is a Norwegian-American physicist who shared the Nobel Prize in Physics in 1973 with Leo Esaki and Brian Josephson "for their discoveries regarding tunnelling phenomena in solids" Giaever's share of the prize was specifically for his "experimental discoveries regarding tunneling phenomena in superconductors".[2] Giaever is a professor emeritus at the Rensselaer Polytechnic Institute, a professor-at-large at the University of Oslo, and the president of the company Applied Biophysics.

As part of the 62nd Lindau Nobel Laureate Meeting, Giaever commented on the significance of the apparent rise in temperature when he stated, "What does it mean that the temperature has gone up 0.8 degrees Kelvin: probably nothing." Referring to the selection of evidence in his presentation, Giaever stated "I pick and choose when I give this talk just the way the previous speaker (Mario Molina) picked and chose when he gave his talk." Giaever concluded his presentation with a pronouncement: "Is climate change pseudoscience? If I'm going to answer the question, the answer is: absolutely."

Giaever repeated his claims in a speech at the same place in 2015: "The American Physical Society, which I was a member, say that "the evidence is incontrovertible", that global warming exists. Now think about that. This is a physical society and they say you cannot discuss global warming, because we believe it's happening. It's like the Catholic Church. There are lots of incontrovertible truth in the Catholic Church some sure. And here are incontrovertible truth in a physical society. So the only answer to that is to resign and I resigned in 11 A main point of Giaever's speech was discussing reliability of the statistical calculation of this temperature with respect to the spatial distribution of measurement locations over the globe, especially what he viewed as poor coverage in the southern hemisphere and Arctic.

Giaever is currently a science advisor with American conservative and libertarian think tank, The Heartland Institute.

Interestingly , Giaever is an atheist.

I am not, but I am a Catholic and reside in Lake Leelanu, Michigan.